Lucy's Kids and Money Saving Tips

By Lucille Tyler Baldwin

Author of the

Financially Fabulous Divas series

The day will come when our children will move out of our homes and be required to make financial decisions for themselves, such as buying or renting a place to live, buying a car, purchasing life and property insurance, starting and taking care of a family, and more.

The pressing question that we must ask ourselves is, "Have we prepared them for the real world?"

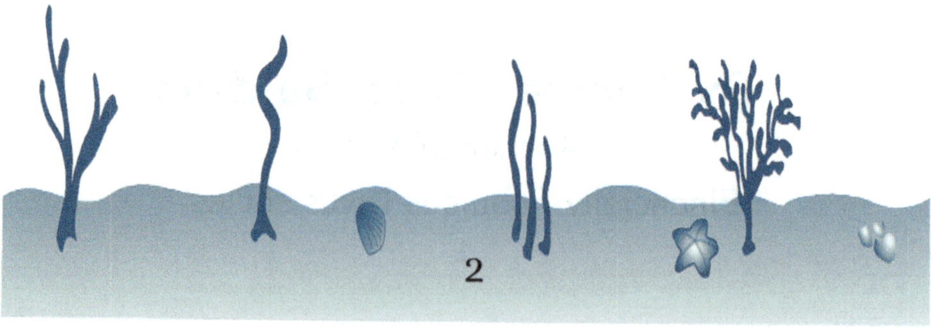

Ann Landers said it best…

"It is not what you do for your children, but what you have prepared them to do for themselves, that will make them successful human beings."

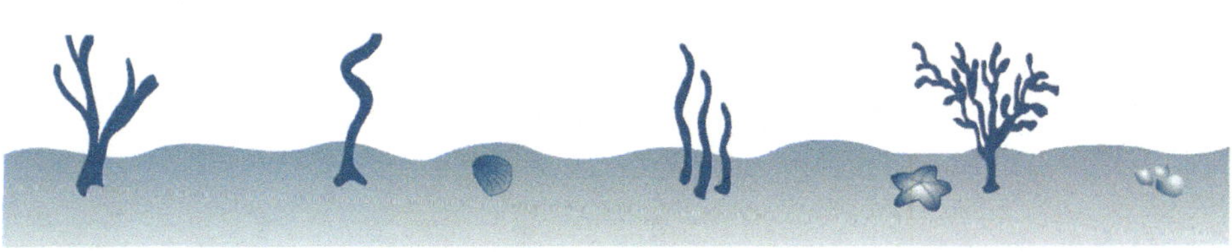

Hi! My name is Victoria. I have always wanted to have fins. So, my nana used her magical pen to turn me into a beautiful mermaid. Now I can help you with this book.

That is my cousin, Nicholas. I do not know why he is here.

I want to learn how to save money too, Victoria!

Why is it important to learn how to save and make good choices with money?

Because if you spend all the money that you receive from special occasions such as birthdays, holidays, and money from doing chores or even your allowance...

you will probably waste a lot of money!

If you learn how to save and set financial goals,

you are more likely to have money available when you need it most.

You can set short, medium or long-term goals.

Examples of Short-Term Goals:

- Saving for a video game
- Saving for a book.
- Saving for a birthday present.
- Saving for extra school supplies, etc.

Examples of Medium-Term Goals:

- Saving for holiday gifts.
- Saving for a new bike.
- Saving for a class trip.
- Saving for a new video game console.

Examples of Long-Term Goals:

1. Saving for a car
2. Saving for higher education.
3. Saving for a house.
4. Saving for a wedding.
5. Saving for a family.
6. Saving for retirement.

By learning to save and set financial goals you will not become dependent on other people for money when you get older.

Saving just a little money consistently will add up over time. For example, if you save just $1.37 a day for a year you will have

$500.00.

Saving money means learning the difference between a **NEED and a WANT.**

We need things such as...

- **food**
- **shelter**
- **clothes**
- **and water**

We sometimes **WANT** things that
we consider needs:
but we can survive without items
such as...

fast food
junk food
video consoles/games
trendy shoes and clothes
flavored drinks

It is important to understand the value of the things that you buy.

Try not to spend a lot of money on things that have little or no financial value.

Some items such as fast food have no financial value, because once you consume/eat the food - the food is gone and so is your **money**!

Clothes and shoes are also items that have little value once you use/wear them.

How much do you think those $200.00 sneakers are worth after you have worn them for a few months? Even the coolest gadgets will eventually go down in value.

It is wise to spend some of your money on things that will hold their value or go up in value. When something goes up in value it **appreciates**.

Items that increase in value or have financial worth are called **assets**.

You can exchange assets for money. When you exchange assets for cash it is called liquidating.

Some assets have fancy names,

but

they are simply different ways to save or invest money.

Some examples of assets are...

Savings Accounts

U.S. Savings Bonds

Certificates of Deposit (CD's)

Mutual Funds

Money Market Accounts

IRA's

Property/Real Estate, Gold, etc.

A Savings Account is where you deposit money for safe keeping.

Did you know that you can start saving and investing for college or a trade school long before you are ready to go? It costs a lot of money to attend college.

Kid's Money Club

Another way to save money is to buy U.S. Savings Bonds. When you buy U.S. Savings Bonds, you are lending the government money.

After a certain period
(when the bond matures),
the government will repay the loan
and pay you extra money called
interest.

You can buy U.S. Savings Bonds for
as little as $25.00.

A **Certificate of Deposit**, also known as a CD, is another way to save money.

A **(CD)** is a time deposit account, which means you must leave the money in the bank for a set amount of time, usually 3, 6, or 9 months or longer.

A **Money Market Account** is a savings account that normally requires about $500 -$2500 to open.

That is because money market accounts normally pay higher interest rates than regular savings accounts.

A Mutual Fund consists of many people (called investors) putting their money together to buy assets such as stocks, bonds, or other securities.

A Mutual Fund Manager takes the money and combines it with other investors' money to buy a diverse mix of **investments**.

For example, you can invest or buy shares of stock in a company that serves your favorite fast food or

own a piece of the company that makes and sells the shoes that you are wearing.

When people get older, they may want to stop working. When you stop working you will still need money to pay bills, buy food, clothes and other necessities.

In order to have money when you retire, it is important to start saving and investing while you are young.

It is getting late and my mother is calling me for dinner. But before I go, I want to tell you about retirement accounts.

There are different types of RETIREMENT ACCOUNTS.

Retirement accounts are special accounts that allow young adults to start saving money early and over a long period of time.

The 3 most common long-term retirement accounts are:

- **A 401(K)**

  A 401(K) is a retirement plan through your employer/job. Your employer may also contribute money to your savings.

Next you have **IRAs**
(Individual Retirement Account)

- **Roth IRA**

  A Roth IRA is a retirement plan that has a tax-free structure if you meet certain requirements.

- Traditional IRA

  A Traditional IRA is a personal savings plan for your retirement.

Remember you are never too young to start saving and investing for your future. Ernie's mom and dad can get an early start and begin planning for his financial future while he is a baby.

Be sure to learn or accomplish something every day that will move you one step closer to your goals.

Glossary

Allowance

To receive a sum of money regularly.

Appreciate

Increase in value.

Consistently

To do always/regularly.

Diverse

Many different types.

Invested

To put money into something hoping to earn more money.

Loan

Borrowed money that is expected to be paid back with interest.

Pay Yourself First

Put a little money in your savings account before spending on anything else.

Stock

Money/Capital raised by a company by selling shares.

Waste

To use carelessly.

Lucy's Kids and Money the book series includes:

Lucy's Kids and Money: Credit

Lucy's Kids and Money: Credit Cards

Lucy's Kids and Money: Financial Mumbo Jumbo

Lucy's Kids and Money: Saving

Lucy's Kids and Money: Basic Taxes

Lucy's Kids and Money: When I Grow Up

Ha ha! Did you think that was the end of the book?

A Secret Underwater Adventure

Let's have some fun!

Word Search

I	A	L	L	O	W	A	N	C	E
N	U	O	W	A	S	T	E	I	E
V	P	Z	N	V	B	P	S	W	D
E	S	U	A	M	H	Y	P	A	O
S	L	O	A	N	L	C	E	N	N
T	M	S	L	U	Q	K	N	T	A
F	G	A	C	K	B	Z	D	X	T
K	A	V	V	N	E	E	D	X	E
P	V	E	R	A	M	B	I	W	U
A	P	P	R	E	C	I	A	T	E

Allowance Appreciate Donate Invest Loan Need

Save Spend Want Waste

Where do fish keep their money?
In a riverbank!

Coloring Fun

Can you help us find our way home?
I knew it! We are lost.

Answer on page 99

Set
Financial Goals

Short-term.
Medium-term,
and
Long-term Goals.

Short-Term Goals

(May take12 months or less)

A Medium-Term Goal

(2 months to 3 years to achieve)

Long-Term Goals

(12 months or more to achieve)

OPEN
I love shopping!

You should not spend all of your money!
But, I needed a new crown!

There is a difference between a Need and a Want.

These are some examples of needs.
Food
Water
Shelter
Clothes

Do You think she should save some money for the future?

Yes______ No_______

What is Consumer Debt?

Consumer Debt

Consumer Debt is money people **BORROW** for personal, family, or household purposes.

Examples of Consumer Debt

- Credit Card Debt
- Student Loans
- Auto Loans
- Mortgages
- Payday Loans
- Medical Bills

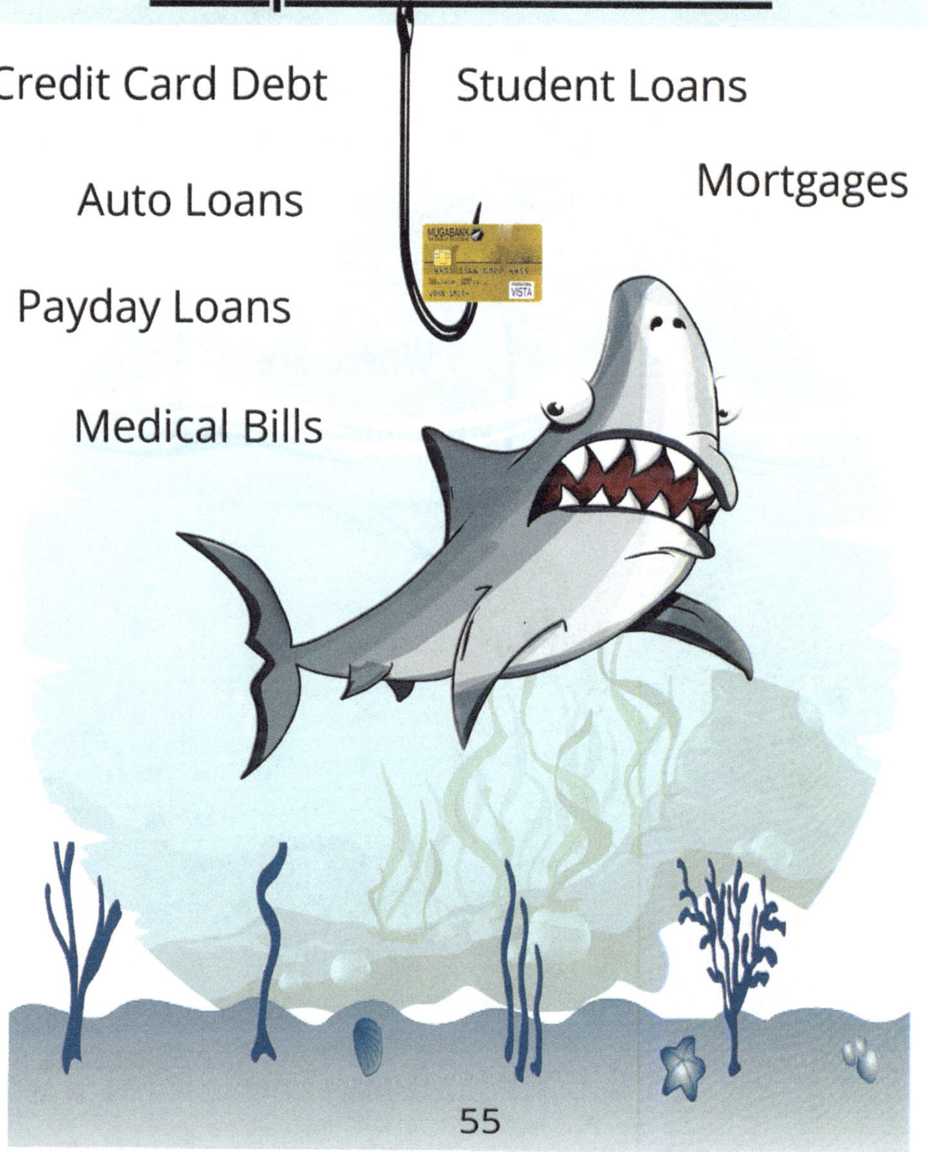

Where are
the money trees?

Money Does Not Grow on Trees

Remember, it is important to learn how to save and plan for the future.
How?

Earn Your Own Money.
Track Your Spending.
Set Saving Goals.
Why shoud I track my spending?

Track Your Spending

When you track your spending, you get a clear picture of where your money is going.

You should learn how to budget.
What is a budget?

A budget helps you plan how to spend and save money.
That makes sense.
Save
Spend
Invest
Donate

True or False

(Circle Your Answer)

Learning to budget can help you build healthy money skills when it comes to spending or saving.

Coloring Break

Why do seahorses live in saltwater?

What has lots of rings but no fingers?
I know! I know!

A
Telephone

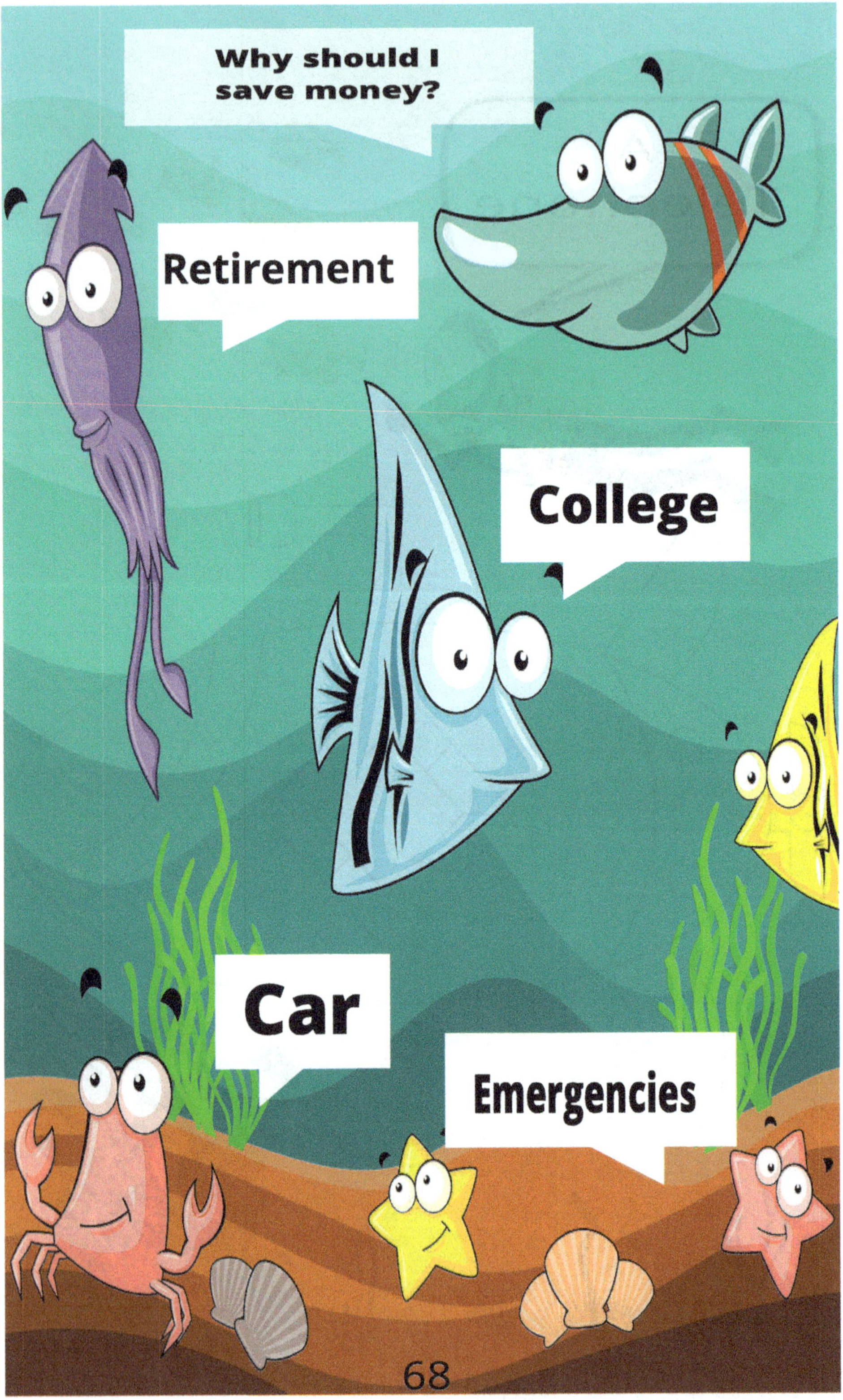
Why should I save money?
Retirement
College
Car
Emergencies

Saving is cool!

Long Term Money Goals Can Help You Prepare For the Future..

Color Me Pretty

Mermaids

How many words can you make from Mermaids?

You are doing a Great Job!
Thank you!

Did You Know?

(Check Your Quarters)

Notes

UNITED STATES OF AMERICA
LIBERTY
IN GOD WE TRUST
QUARTER DOLLAR

Coloring Break

Why don't fish play basketball?

What is your favorite color?

Word Scramble

Word Bank:

Allowance Appreciate Donate Invest Loan Need Save Spend Want Waste

1. EALWLACNO ______________________
2. ETARPAPECI ______________________
3. EATNDO ______________________
4. STVINE ______________________
5. LONA ______________________
6. EDEN ______________________
7. ASVE ______________________
8. DNSPE ______________________
9. WTAN ______________________
10. WSATE ______________________

True or False

(Circle Your Answer)

A budget helps
you plan how to spend and
save your money.

True or False

(Circle Your Answer)

There is a difference between a need and a want?

Keep saving!

Did you know that snails have more teeth than any other animal?

True or False

(Circle Your Answer)

Money grows
on trees?

Did You Know?

Bingo
M
O
N
E
Y

What goes up but never comes down?
Ha ha! Your age!

Draw A Picture of a seahorse.

Did you know the numbers on the clock across add up to 12?

What gets wet while drying?

A Blue Whale's tongue can weigh as much as an ELEPHANT!

I am a Jellyfish.
You are not a fish.

You are a dome-shaped invertebrate. You do not have backbones.

Jellyfish are 95% water!

Jellyfish do not have brains, hearts, blood or gills.

I found
lots of sea
shells by the sea shore.

There really are no money trees!

The figures used are for illustrative purposes.

Lucy's Kids and Money should not be considered financial advice. The purpose of *Lucy's Kids and* Money series is to introduce our kids to basic financial information and to encourage them to start talking and asking questions about money.

Author of the Financially Fabulous Divas series
Financiallyfabulousdivas@gmail.com

Made in the USA
Monee, IL
03 November 2026

67379271R00056